ALSO BY DAVID FISHER

Requiem for Heurtubrise (ManRoot) 1974
The Most Wanted Man in America (Stein & Day) 1975
Teachings (Back Roads Press) 1978

THE BOOK OF MAD-NESS

POEMS BY
DAVID FISHER

COLLAGES BY
GEORGE HITCHCOCK

APPLE-WOOD PRESS

CAMBRIDGE/NEWTON   1980

ACKNOWLEDGMENTS

This book was originally published in 1975 by Gallimaufry. The author would like to thank Mary MacArthur, former editor and publisher of Gallimaufry books.

Some of these poems first appeared in the following journals: *Kayak, BackRoads, ManRoot, Gallimaufry, The Wisconsin Review,* and *The Paris Review.*

The Book of Madness © 1975, 1980 David Fisher

ISBN: 0-918222-16-8 hardcover

POEMS BY
DAVID FISHER

THE BOOK OF MAD- NESS

COLLAGES BY
GEORGE HITCHCOCK

For Amanda Who Waited
For Tlaloc Who Died

CONTENTS

If the road leading you to your liberation is that of disease, of lies, of dishonor, it is then your duty to plunge into disease, into lies, into dishonor, that you may conquer them. You may not otherwise be saved.

Kazantzakis, *The Saviors of God*

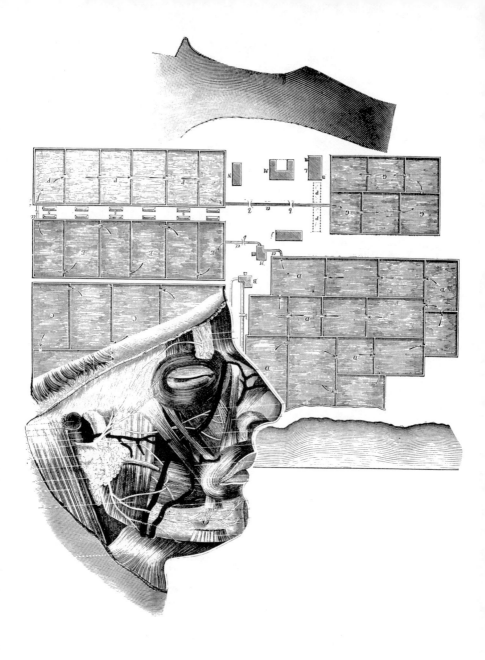

THE ROLLER COASTER
Adapted from the Spanish of Nicanor Parra

During the past
fifty years
  (Hell, during any
  past fifty years)
poetry
was a spa
for solemn fools.

Then we came along
with our roller coaster.

Get on, if you choose.

But we won't do a thing
if you get off,
bleeding theoretical blood

at the mouth and nose.

LOST

The bare room,
the table cries,
the doctors harvest the silver vertebrae.
The restraints are terrifying.

"Perhaps you have made of death,"
says the doctor,
"an idea excessively false."

A strange clear dream is born to the poet
in the isolation room.
The doctor is wearing
a nacre and ebony serpent.
The shackled celestial poet
opens the violet of his heart—
forgetfulness uproots the symphony—
a star is feeding.
There is angel strife in the poet's eyes,
o little lost poet with
many fine doctors and one celestial pillow.

from AMANDA'S MUSIC

I cannot control the hallucinations.
I describe an arc
about my throat with a razor.

The blood runs down my shirt
and spills
over the buckle. Someone borrows
a dime from me
to call.

*   *   *   *   *

In Tubingen
a willow bends
towards the river, where
the Hölderlin tower
is gold in the moonlight,
there Hölderlin, in his madness
wrote scraps of verse
on freshly-planed boards...

*   *   *   *   *

...& Rimbaud, in his final delirium,
made an inventory of the ivory which
he had longed to possess:
"Item: one tusk
Item: two tusks
Item: three tusks."

*   *   *   *   *

My students have taken over the train
in Yugoslavia.
I must remember their names or die.
Two border guards enter
our compartment armed with submachine guns.
I am afraid they have come for my wife.
I attack them.
They can tell it is an American, &
they leave. I have a seizure,
and fall off the train.

*   *   *   *   *

15

The white wind rides cold off the sea

    my sanity is hideous
your eyelids are patterned
        in chevrons

the walls are hung in blue
I am afraid to see my room
        or you
The moon is hidden, and the white wind
      picks its way
   through foghorns.

        * * * * *

The chair was in a painful room, a room
without a dog. The Terror
of the chair. Its punctuation scrambled,
lacking any quilt.

        * * * * *

Streets were ending around him.
He became afraid his street would end.
He speeded up.

    His street ended
against a black warehouse
and he turned left quickly
following the tracks.

        * * * * *

Blue cornflower, and mandrake,
the tomb of the king.
The monkish litany of the wind.
Dusk came, with a strange light,
to Giza......
        In the grey night
        the star of the pharaoh
        overtook him.
        He descended in sleep
        to his sister.

I CUT MY THROAT
WITH AN EASY MOTION

I cut my throat with an easy motion;
my intent had been to blot out the fake green
leaves of the plants, complete to the last serration,
my intent had been to submerge the boat
that rides the green hills of the Blue Ridge Mountains.
  But by now it was winter in Munich,
and my God, I was crying, and the beams of my lamps
had caught the gold eyes of a fox.

I followed the fox across the frozen snow.

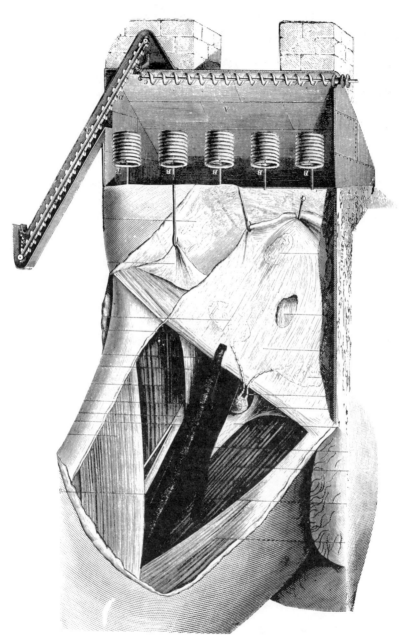

MARVIN GARDENS

Hotels are red.
                     Houses are green.
But what color is Marvin Gardens?
He cupped his head and spilled
      blank orange dice.

$50s are blue.
             And $100s...?

Above him the hospital finished its pivot
and all the spiders changed color.

THE STRAIT JACKET

Pain is tight with images
the broken world
the unrecited world...

The canvas tight
about your chest,
no dream goes free—
and what unfolding can there be?

Let them say this:
That you knew how to flower in these bonds,
that you became some monstrous fruit:
Let them say
The Lord discovered you one day
wrapped all in madness, and aflame.

20

AGE

She naps.
The voice of the wind.
The stones lie glittering before her.
Somewhere a beetle drones.

Something is missing,
perhaps a button,
or the Lord's name.
They have taken her piece of glass.

So little is possible.
Ping-pong and evacuation are separate.

All this confusion.

And still, sometimes,
the whole Blue Ridge is moving in her eyes.

THE BIRDS OF ARLES

But what is happening I see
around us a jungle
of furniture begin to enlarge itself
the Morris chair is growing

roots and vines form in a

vegetal exuberance
behind the hedge

Almost as high as my shoulders
vines of string beans undulate
and outside the house a thousand birds
have rented the telephone wires

and I (reading lips) see a laugh
which I take for the sound of birds
of those birds of the asylum at Arles
which speak during the mistral from
the immobile plane trees

After ten shocks I heard
a lovely phrase repeated by
the birds of Arles:

"Would you and Tlaloc like to go
for a ride in the country?"
We were overjoyed, but before
I could reply I was mad
rolling again through vacant space
past the tribunals
of innumerable silent judges

I returned slowly to the world
to find the invitation
(from the birds of Arles)
was no longer current.

ELECTROSHOCK

O rubber mouthpiece
o tremor that brailles my heart
the frail gymnastics
of my jigging limbs
Desire, the tiger,
rolls in the flame of the cord...

I lie on many hills
the doors swing open
birds are screaming
History is mercifully lost—

and fresh headlamps have come to comb my wall.

THE PARANOID

I
was abandoned.
The birds
disappeared.
There was
no sound.
The days
were warmer.
The valley
was far.

Please
let me live.

YOUR HAIR IS WET WITH THE FOG

Your wall.
And the hospital guards your refusal to speak,
the evident symmetry of your silence.
Small birds play near you
in the garden.
You are the fullness of my desire,
where beasts and planets roll.

Your silence renders me clumsy.
Perhaps you have already understood
the little I know.

Yet I try to tell you,
and you are secret,
your resolution is not to be hurt,
and our madness allows us no tears.

My sleep is troubled
by an astonishing love
which you organize.

And I am trembling
in this wretched hospital, I have no hiding place
your hair is wet with the fog
and my love for you
is a river of trembling hands.

FULTON STREET

Tonsils of fog/
    glass bones of the moon.
The cats trot close/
    to the buildings.
He is dreaming...
    of tapers burning softly
    of the sweet smell of greasewood
    of young girls,
       their bodies smooth
        and bitter gold.
Some trick of the window
sounds like a mourning dove,
    which calls him to the present:
ragged cats
       trot close to the buildings,
      telephone poles are swaying

          in the wind.

THE SEAHORSE

My mouth working with the drug, I
watch the seahorse for hours, rehearse
the movement of its tiny mandibles
with mine. A man is looking at the
manatee, and I inform him that it
eats water hyacinths, and is
extinct in Indonesia. He is noncommittal.

I pass into the zoo. My ears
are so acute I can hear the wings
of insects. I strike up a conversation
with a young girl and inform her that
the average aphid gives birth every
ninety minutes. The girl moves on.

The pigmy hippopotamus is under
water, except for his nose, he does not
appear to be in the mood, so I move on
to the beavers. I am feeling *rotten*.
I take off my belt, the llamas
watch me intently as I tighten it,
and tap the dropper home, the rush
distends the veins in my ears.

Once more I am full of love and
information, but no one appears to
notice, except the macaque and the
North American Sociable Vulture.
I recite Rilke's poem about the leopard.

A keeper appears to be watching me,
and I tell him why the polyphemus moth
displays false eyes on its wings,
and I do my marmot imitation, but he is
unimpressed. I move on, and observe
that the one-armed man is also watching me.

I quicken my pace. Now I look back,
and the okapi are following me. I break
into a run. Small tattling birds call out
my coordinates as I plunge through the woods.
The giraffes are thundering behind me,
I hear the tramp of camels and the screams
of the wild dogs. I am terribly frightened.

At last I vault the fence and stand,
breathless, outside the zoo. On the
windshield of my car a ticket flutters.

THE TORMENT

My crippled mind
reaches into the sea.
Everywhere there is loss,
the moon is adrift,
the stupid alders breed.

My mind which would be bright
and smooth
is a shipwreck of horses.

My vision contracts
my limbs are spars
I hate the pendulous filth
of the willow.

I have neither power nor wisdom.
Today I am pregnant with husks.

George Hitchcock

REHEARSAL

The far faint protocols of Katherine's flute
drip from the eucalyptus, in the rain.
Sleepy birds, with songs in their eyes, are mute;
sheep on the hillside dream of sun-warmed stones.
      Beyond a lighted window in the night
      bone-weary folk consider Henry's plight.

Messengers come and go in the struggling eyes
of the small dog on the hearth, who feebly whines
at death scenes, barks when Gloucester dies—
his old eyes struggle to retain their lines.
      Splash of a mailed fist against its sword,
      an ancient syntax gathers with each word.

A cow peers in the window, stands amazed
to see the slaughtering reach of human loins.
Was this the ensanguined end for which cows grazed?
She belches lightly, her eyes spin like coins.
      Rumination cannot tell her what to say
      to hecatombs of a Shakespearean play.

WHY DO YOU WANT TO SUFFER LESS

I go to school.
My new duality arranges her skirts
between tricks.
The intellect is the cigarette
that makes me hungry.

Dragged-in terminologies,
obese fogs ready for frying,
My mind, inflamed, bloats on distinctions,
the future becomes a monotonous instrument.

Decorous poetry.
Good wives peopled
       with swallows—
          bituminous rivers.

My thoughts,
trained to bifurcate like a seal,
are a form of sewage.

       "I thought there were some
       nice plays on sound—'video'
       and 'fidelity.'"

       "I picked up a sense of penetration
       through repression."

I can no longer reply
with one green word.
I am ready for shock.
My mind has lips like a claymore.
My mind is a whore.
My mind has murdered my suffering.

SONG OF THE NEEDLE

The moon lies on the horizon like a bird.
Locusts die on the cowl of our plane,
their bones interned on the dark floor
of the paperweight.

The cornborer warns of frost.

How we fear
the dance of the fire-dogs,
o Lord,
      their saurian prints
are the architects of morning...

Among fierce asters
still we seek
the soft white poppy.

I am a slow derelict, with enormous feet.

THE BOXCAR

a boxcar rolled
through the night
    it slowed
    and stopped

there were whispering noises
as the spiders rolled back
    the doors

the low moon passed through the
open car/   like a spear

    the spiders descending
were like a blue afghan
under the moon

IN LITTLE ROCK

In Little Rock
on blazing nights
through evenings
freckled with profanity
we hear the thrum
of the jew's-harp.
There is a dung beetle
rolling past
like a child
with a hoop.
(heat lightning dreams
like a wurlitzer...)
There is an old man
who sometimes wears
different shoes
and sometimes the same.
Stars are dim
        as seed pearls,
gauze-winged bats
move round
the yellow moon.
I make a run
to E. 11th Street
for some Jet Malt Liquor,
when I return
        a large pale scorpion
        is dead in my room.

THE EMERGENCY ROOM

Chic desolation of the
factory—a rigid girl
is carrying someone's lunch.
An old man is bleeding
in a plastic chair.
Small doctors
in Hush Puppies pass
like clam diggers waving
from the meridian beach.
An old man is bleeding,
he is bleeding the rich rust orange
of the Pacific Fruit Express.
There are icicles of blood
on his chin.
He is saying, *"Brutos.*
Brutos. **Savages.**
Sooner or later you going
to pay for it."

"What's the problem, sir?"
someone asks.
The old man looks up, for a moment
his eyes are black.
"Oh," he says. "Many problem..."
He becomes frightened,
unable to finish his sentence.

THE SERPENT GOD

After school he would
fill his pockets with
mice from the stables
and climb
        the meadow
where the belled cows grazed.
When he neared the cave
his pockets began to squirm.

      He sat in the cave and listened
to the sound of bees in the meadow
and the little shrieks
of the mice.

      It was almost dark
at the mouth
      of the cave.
A cow made a dull clinking sound.
The moccasin stirred beside him.

Outside in the meadow
there were fireflies
    ●●●●●●●●●●●●●

THE OLD ONES

The old ones
the sachems
are skulls in the desert
sand blows over
the feathered spear.
Now the snake ripples
past trembling flowers
over baked and cracking
                              clay.
I am the dog with
the broken back
crawling across
the mesa of sorrow,
I am the cross of bones,
the badger wears me
on his finger

        in the fields of lightning.

A JUNKIE WITH A FLUTE IN THE RAIN

A child with a wrench is
moving through Harlem, turning
on the hydrants. A junkie howls
at a bus stop, and a drunk
with a beer in a small paper bag
does a two-step outside Minnie's.
Venus rises from the tenements,
Priapus weighs his sex in the scale
against a nickel bag
(And you must come to see me)
Here street lights pray over the avenues
like Giacometti nuns,
pigeons are thin as sparrows,
the roaches big as grapes. Old ladies
sit in hotel lobbies in chairs
chained to the walls. On park benches
old men are stacked
like doves on a telephone wire.

Origami birds nest in my room
beside a sculpture
made of broken needles
and you must come to see me
you will find me, love, in the streets

a junkie with a flute in the rain

ANALYST

Picking through pieces
one cannot spare space or memory
in the great dustbin where illness must be lost
Outside the hands of the furniture
the thick half-dream of the client

> *one is tired*
> *one is in pain*
> *one confuses essential facts*

The desperate empty eye confronts you—
the empty indigo of a blind window.
Body deserted by sleep,
tomb of deliberate servitude,
pure lack of human franchise.

And yet, o psychiatric fidelity
o weary love with a cigarette
o vulnerable delicate question small
as a hole in a bone.

The client is trembling with cold,
without your identity he slows,
repeats himself—and you must summon again
the steady, weary magic of sortilege.

Your dream is of silence
your hands are of leaves
the straw
at the edge of the sky calls your name.

o dear Lord forgive the healer,
whose words are as mixed with comfort and terror
as rain on the sea.

A MAJESTIC OLD GENTLEMAN

A majestic old gentleman, smelling of
pigs' feet, hailed me at
    88th and East 14th &
  got in the front seat backwards,
      with his head towards
      the windshield and his legs
      thrown over the seat.

"Turn this cab around," he said. "We're
going the wrong way." So I
    hung a U and we sped off
      to the Faith Deliverance Center.

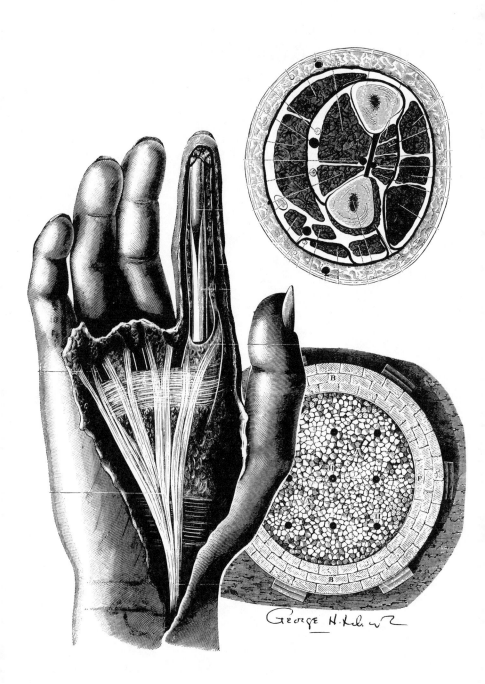

George H. Kolowski

THE POET SALUTES HIS MALADY
adapted from the French of Jean Cocteau

Salut good malady
o blessed malady o chamber
of illness, bed of justice,
throne of the king.

Salut o wall of written cries
Thanks great prison open
to witness against me.

In the evening we see fly
the wing that was coiled
in the forehead of the conscript
we see a Christ coiffed with swallows
a Christ crowned with the cries of birds

Rose to the right of my bed
lips made up by the sun
a drole overture to surrounding maternality
(I am afraid to learn where you are—
black irises brandishing pistillate sex)
Rose neither red nor black
watered with flows of blood
from my meagre body
you erect with impudence
high on your spiny neck
your profound small mouth

NOSTALGIA
translated from the Italian of
Giuseppe Ungaretti

When
the night
is vanishing
a little before the spring
and it's rare
that anyone passes

over Paris
grows thick
a dark color
of weeping

In the corner
of a bridge
I contemplate
the limitless silence
of a slender girl.

Our maladies
are fused.

And, as though carried away,—
we remain.

THE MUTILATED SOLDIER

The torches surrounded by butterflies,
the fox fulfills a long dream of rapine,
his tail is on fire, the tail of his brothers
are on fire—the pale wheat is in flames.

In this year of the luminous horloge, the year of the grand interior
flame,
a soldier also seeks to avoid
his Emperor's service, by mutilating
the two great fingers of his hand.

The mutilated soldier
his crown cold with roses
assumes the burden of the fox.
He speaks to a crow, to a silly goose.
He says confusing tender words
to the beasts,
The mutilated Soldier.

TO THE FATES
translated from the German of
Friedrich Hölderlin

One more summer grant, you powerful ones!
And an autumn, to ripen my song,
That more willingly my heart, from the
Sweet play sated, might die.

The Soul, that in life has not
Received her right, is restless below.
But if once the holy thing
that lies at my heart, might succeed in the Poem,

Welcome then, o stillness of the shadow-world!
I am at peace, though I should descend
without my lyre;   once
I lived like the gods, and more is not needed.

MADNESS IS A FRESCO

Madness is a fresco
by Orozco, Siqueiros,
full of colors, gaily wound
with whips, of stone or fire,
and fine inquisitors.
But there is no weeping,
      no weeping!

Madness is a fresco
by Rivera
with lion's teeth, and biting arrows
and luscious fruit, and funny faces.
But there is no grief,
      no grief!

When the mad go out,
the wind is dead,
cold homes laid by,
their misty faces pressing at your window.

THE RETARDED CLASS
AT F.A.O. SCHWARZ'S
CELEBRATES CHRISTMAS

Mr. Klein says, "Milagres, hold Angelo's hand,"
So I do, and we walk past a million toys.
I especially like the blue ones.
When I sit on Santa's knee, I
Hold to Angelo's hand, and try to
Think of a good thing to ask.
At last I ask Santa
If I can come back next year.
I am not sure I have earned a blue one.

THE VIETNAMESE GIRL
IN THE MADHOUSE:
For Thai Tran

Someone's youngest daughter
has lost her mind, there is
more meaning in a snail's cuneiform
than in her prattle in three tongues,
still she is lovely
with her hair loosed;
and only beside the bones of these hills
is she ever silent, can she ever be silent,
and we are too poor for her madness.

PAIN

Outside the church,
the gulls are like grain.
He kneels and prays for his pain,
he prays from the Armed Forces Hymnal.
Too lazy for entire candour,
still he confesses.
As he talks, his pain
    turns a long screw softly,
    precisely edits its bite.
His daughter is also mad,
the red horse is loosed,
He kisses the warm bronze feet
of Mary.

Outside the church,
the gulls are like grain.

CONFUSION

"You got two milks?" the old man asked.
He could see the window of his Plymouth.

An old man shaves as long as he can.
"You got two milks?" he asked. "Two milks?"

He couldn't work his Plymouth through the window
though the window worked.

An old man sleeps as long as he can.
His milk was in the Plymouth.

"You got two milks?" the old man asked.
He could see his Plymouth from the window.

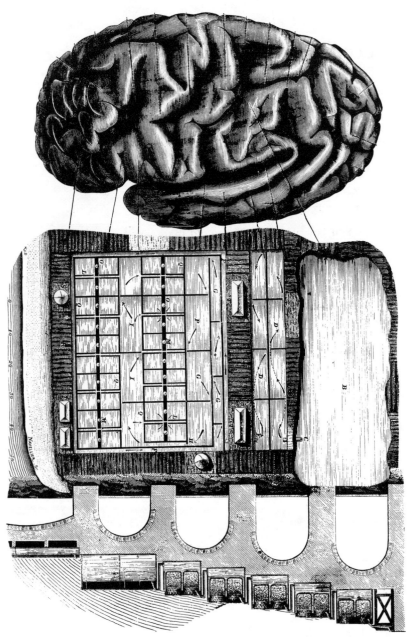

George Hitchcock

THE TEACHER

When I was a teacher
I taught the students that
the two great levelers are
Pestilence and Disease, and then
a few days later I would ask the students
what the two great levelers are,
and they would answer, "Disease
and Pestilence," and I would lose
my temper, and roar, "No, that
is wrong, it is Pestilence and Disease."
They were hopeless. And I would teach them
the structure of tragedy, and I would
diagram the structure on the blackboard, thus:

They did not understand, some
did not even copy down the diagram.

*

I have retired, now, to my father's
small stump farm. I eat cress, berries, cattail sprouts,
and chives, but mostly mushrooms: orange chanterelles
and Zeller's boletus that I gather in gunny sacks.
I fry them, boil them, broil them, pickle them, and
eat them raw. They make me somewhat dizzy.
I wear a miner's helmet,
Still I have bad dreams.

*

The hogs crowd round the stove,
a possum hangs from the hall tree.
Under the cabin, goats browse
the dynamite. A new spring came up in a field
and I took a shovel
and I tried to coax it
nearer the house, but it dived
down a badger hole and disappeared.

*

I have put up chintz curtains. In the
appalling heat, under the socket moon,
I worm the corn. When I was a student
I went to Wales, to Mynydd Llanybyther, and Cwmpidlfach,
I stayed with Thurlow Craig, who told me
country stories, of the dance of the stoats,
of rooks who breed on the midden, of the fox
who played dead to catch the buzzard.
At night we visited the local
In a cart drawn by a pedigreed Cardigan cob.

I make my own beer now, with
good English malt, I add the hops
in an old stocking my wife left. Sometimes
the hydrometer tells me it is thirty proof,
sometimes, in the moonlight,
a bottle explodes, rattling the windows.

*

It is winter,
the landscape is set forth
like the best blue china.

A young frost makes her
first sketches on the
panes of my cabin.

Someday I should like to teach again.

Outside, on the cold roof of my Nash,
I hear the frosty clatter of goat hooves.

BURY THE DEAD

Fright of the caribou behind his floe.
The hunter's arms are long and blind,
the noiseless J of his paddle,
shadow of the bow,
the splash of the final baptism.

O forget the dead,
forget your own cheerleader whirling in gold
forget the backs broken by the *cortito*,
the terrible mask of the moon
the impassable bridge of yellow stars.

Bury the dead, bury death, bury even
the lunar surface of death.

For three antelopes, the mother, the father
the baby are working their way across
the Wyoming plains.

Gently they receive the rain, for you, like a white
cotillion.

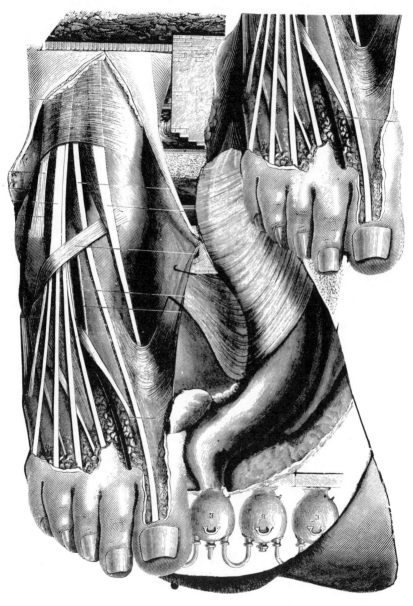

George Hitchcock

IN YOUTH

In youth I was eager to observe
the movements of dying dogs,
the rings of moss on the keel of
swamped boats, the way old women
knot their scarves.

When sleep was denied me
I listened to the winds in the
orchard.

Headlong I rushed past the antique
bazaars, pausing only to eat a
slice of cold melon sold from a
truck.

Now I cried for what was irretrievably
lost, and determined not to have another child.
I trembled in my grief like a cypress,
cold in the paradise of autumn.

CANTA DEL BORRACHON
EN GUADALAJARA

The overhead fans
spun
in the heat
like stagecoach wheels.
The drunk was
weeping,
holding up a sparerib.
Everything had to be explained
to him: the light, the flies.

The bartenders took turns
explaining to him,
the light, the flies.
Their dark eyes flickered
    over their maguey kingdom.
He wept on a shoebox.
like a little cold horse,
he poured a Superior over his shoulder.

What impressed me was
his will to understand.

    He asked everyone.

He ordered tequila,
and stood alone,
in a bar,
in this city of discarded limes.

It began to thunder.
Ghosts of cool rain
sprang through the swinging doors.
The drunk was holding up
a sparerib, weeping.

Through the wings of the doors
I saw, in the rain,
the dark hair of a girl.

The Apple-wood Press began in January 1976.
The image of the apple joined with the hard
concreteness of wood in many ways expresses the goals of
the press. One of the first woods used in printing, apple-
wood remains a metaphor for giving ideas a form. Apple-
wood Press books are published in the memory of Harry
and Lillian Apple.